W9-DIU-547

COMMUNITY WORKERS

A Mail Carrier's Job

MIGUEL ROSARIO

Cavendish
Square

New York

Published in 2015 by Cavendish Square Publishing, LLC
243 5th Avenue, Suite 136, New York, NY 10016

Library of Congress Cataloging-in-Publication Data

Rosario, Miguel.
A mail carrier's job / Miguel Rosario.
pages cm. — (Community workers)
Includes index.
ISBN 978-1-62712-999-2 (hardcover) ISBN 978-1-62712-351-8 (paperback) ISBN 978-1-62712-352-5 (ebook)
1. Letter carriers—Juvenile literature. I. Title.

HE6241.R67 2015
383.023—dc23

2014001533

Editorial Director: Dean Miller
Editor: Amy Hayes
Copy Editor: Cynthia Roby
Art Director: Jeffrey Talbot
Designer: Douglas Brooks
Photo Researcher: J8 Media
Production Manager: Jennifer Ryder-Talbot
Production Editor: David McNamara

The photographs in this book are used by permission and through the courtesy of: Cover photo by Peter Dazeley/Photographer's Choice/Getty Images; Tetra Images/SuperStock, 5; Bloomberg/Bloomberg/Getty Images, 7; Jonathan Alpeyrie/Polaris/Newscom, 9; © Kim Karpeles/Alamy, 11; © Michael Owen Baker/ZUMA Press, 13; Pimnana_01/Shutterstock.com, 15; Tetra Images/SuperStock, 17; Flying Colours Ltd/Photodisc/Getty Images, 19; Kyle Monk/Blend Images/SuperStock, 21.

Contents

Who I Am 4

Sorting the Mail 6

Using the Mailbox 14

Saying "Hello" 18

Words to Know 22

Find Out More 23

Index 24

I am a **mail carrier**.

Mail carriers bring mail to people's homes.

5

I start my day at the **post office**.

I get to the post office early
to sort out the mail.

7

I **load** the mail into the mail truck.

There is a lot of mail today!

I park my mail truck on the street.

I put some of the mail in my **mail cart.**

I put cards and letters into
the **mailbox.**

13

The red flag on this mailbox is up.

This means that there is mail to pick up.

Sometimes I go to **apartment buildings.**

There are a lot of mailboxes for all the people who live there.

I slide the mail into the right box.

17

Sometimes I hand people their mail.

I stop and say, "Hello."

I like bringing mail to people.

I like being a mail carrier.

21

Words to Know

apartment buildings (a-**part**-ment **bil**-dings) buildings in which many different families live

load (**lohd**) to put something into something else

mailbox (**mayl**-boks) a box where mail is placed

mail carrier (**mayl kayr**-ee-er) a person who brings and picks up mail

mail cart (**mayl kart**) a bag with wheels used to hold mail

post office (**pohst aw**-fis) a place where mail is sorted

Find Out More

Books

Delivering Your Mail
by Ann Owen, Capstone

Mail Carriers at Work
by Karen Latchana Kenney, Magic Wagon

The Post Office Book: Mail and How It Moves
by Gail Gibbons, HarperCollins Children's Books

Website

Let's Go! Learning Adventures
letsgo4preschool.sdcoe.net/content/eng_postoffice.asp

23

Index

apartment building, 16, 22

load, 8, 22

mailbox, 12, 14, 16, 22

mail carrier, 4, 20, 22

mail cart, 10, 22

post office, 6, 22